Gellar Studies
Erik Fuhrer

SPUYTEN DUYVIL
NEW YORK CITY

Library of Congress Cataloging-in-Publication Data

Names: Fuhrer, Erik, author.
Title: Gellar studies / Erik Fuhrer.
Description: New York City : Spuyten Duyvil, [2023]
Identifiers: LCCN 2023012943 | ISBN 9781959556350 (paperback)
Subjects: LCGFT: Poetry.
Classification: LCC PS3606.U395 G45 2023 | DDC 811/.6--dc23/eng/20230331
LC record available at https://lccn.loc.gov/2023012943

INTRODUCTION

I'll put it simply: with *Gellar Studies*, Erik Fuhrer has invented a shining new genre. *Gellar Studies* is an ode and a love letter and a manifestation of that parasocial identification with a singular actor-celebrity that emerges from the magic of that affect from watching, admiring, and empathically identifying as Fuhrer does with Gen X queen Sarah Michelle Gellar. Not only that, but the particular texture familiar to those queer bodies who see something of themselves in their loved one on screen, whether in fiction or fact, most often giving them the correlative to what they hadn't yet been able to name swirling within them.

The poems in *Gellar Studies* are luminous and elegant, expanding the relational duet to include not only Fuhrer's empathic attachment to Gellar as a figure but also all the bodies she lived in through her various roles, the oceans she swam in. What I find most remarkable about Fuhrer's language in these odes, and how they blossom outward, is how Fuhrer communicates the empowerment and pathos a 90s Hollywood starlet can offer a queer and queered body, "I, / no longer me / but a force."

Gellar Studies will be exceptionally delectable and devastating for Gen X LGBTQIA+ readers who are familiar with Gellar's iconic work, but I am confident that any reader will quickly submerge themselves in Fuhrer's stunning, surreal, and powerful waters, hoping to never come up for air.

Addie Tsai, author of *Unwieldy Creatures*

To everyone who read drafts of this book and provided steadfast encouragement. To the incredibly kind baristas at the Blue Bottle where I typed many parts of this book out on my cell phone and who remembered my name and order after my first visit. To the woman who stopped me while I was writing this book to tell me I looked like I stepped out of a Wes Anderson film and had her daughter meet me because she knew she'd love my unicorn shirt. To everyone in Los Angeles who has made me feel so remarkably welcomed as who I am. Who has made me feel like I belong. To everyone who has helped me become the final girl I sometimes never thought I would be—bright and colorful, and confident. To everyone who continually supports me in this becoming.

To all the characters I write to in this book. Especially Helen Shivers and Bridget Kelly. I feel like I know these characters intimately. Like I carry their trauma and deaths with me. I feel like they carry me too. I often caught myself exclaiming, "oh, Helen, I am so deeply sorry." I also heard myself frequently breathing "thank you."

And finally, to Sarah Michelle Gellar, who brought these characters so deeply to life for me that I feel, queerly, like I can talk to them. Like they are part of my life.

CONTENTS

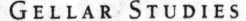

GELLAR STUDIES

My Body Lies Over the Ocean
For Bridget Kelly
Ringer (2011)

I have run
so far
without feathers
that I forget
that somewhere
within my
bones there is
the potential
for flight.
I once tried
to carve wings
into my back
with craft scissors
and slumbered
beneath
a Louboutin
red curve

as you
got lost
in the wet glass
of Tahoe.

In the belly
of you
is a light
that smokes you
into not
recognizing
that you
are glitter.
Gold. I know
that feeling
of smolder
the cooked
remnants
of grief
the way we
doubt who we
are and decide

that poison
is the way
to forgetting.

We can't forget
blood
no matter
how much
it tries
to kill us.
We look
into its eyes
and we
remember
what it
felt like
to be loved.
When they
loved us.
When we
didn't need
wings

to fly. We
just elevated.
Like heat. Blood
is a cold
front. We
become rain.

When younger,
I used to think
the song lyrics
were "my *body*
lies over
the ocean."
And perhaps
mine does. We
are, after all,
mostly water. All
our bodies
fill, spill, flow
elsewhere. Perhaps
that's why
I love

baths. I am
becoming whole
again. This
becomes harder
in a drought.

You thought
you lost
your sister
in the water
and she tried
to scatter you
into rain. Blood.
The cold
blooded killer. I
lost so many
to the rain.
And sometimes
Erik is in
the rain and I
am in
this body.

You too
are split. Answering
to names
that do not
swim within
you. But maybe
if we fake
it enough we
can learn
to love
this strange
new water. We
can baptize
ourselves with new
blood. The blood
we chose. Not
the blood we
were given.

LOCKED INSIDE FOREVER
FOR SARAH MICHELLE GELLAR

In middle school,
I fell
in love
with Sarah
Michelle Gellar.
It wasn't
the lustful,
pin her
poster up
in my locker
kind of
love,
it was the,
wow how
can I
look
as beautiful
as her

kind of
love,
the I
have to pretend
I am
growing my
hair out
because I
want to be
buff
and manly sexy
like a male
wrestler
kind of
love
but I really
want to be
as beautiful
as Buffy
kind of
love.
The painful

I have to
pretend like
I don't
actually admire
her acting,
her clothes,
her wit,
kind of
love.
The be a
fucking
"man"
kind of
love.
The shaming
kind of
love.
The secret
kind of
love.
The love
that wants

to go
shoe shopping
with her
but gets
locked
inside
the store
forever
kind of
love.

When I
was 13,
this kid
I didn't even
know
said he
saw me
kissing
my male
friend at the
lunch table.

That's where
the abuse began.

Kids would
rip off
my backpack,
write "I
am gay"
on it with
chalk. They
tried to dump
me in
the garbage
between bells. My
social studies
teacher
told me
"be a man,"
"fight back."
"I fought
in the war."
"A colonel."

I was a kid
in middle school
whose shoes
never fit.
I did not
enlist.
I did not
resist.

One day, in
chorus, we
were given
free time.
I was working
on my vocab
when another
student asked me
"do you want
to suck
my dick?"
He reached
over

and pulled
the back
of my head
toward him.
Other students
joined, pressing
the back
of my head
toward his
tented pants.
When my
face touched
the fabric
of his jeans,
I swung
my hand.

Apparently, I
was still
holding
my pencil,
and I

slightly punctured
the skin
on his shoulder.

Directly after
my head
was loosened, I
felt him
strike me
across
the face.
I fell off
the folding chair
and he
proceeded
to kick me
repeatedly
about my
body. I
don't remember
how
or when

he stopped.
But I do
remember
not being able
to move.

In the principal's
office I
was asked why
I "stabbed"
this kid
for "no
reason." I
remember
the principal's
smile, when I
told him:
"boys will
be boys,"
he said.
I got three
days in-school

suspension.
The other kid
was given
one day
of lunch detention
for hitting me.

Buffy burnt
down
the gym
to kill
the vampires.
I swung
because the rest
of my body
was not mine
anymore not
in that moment.
I was
a mechanism,
a forward swing
to the rhythm

of shame
and repressed
desire
and the muted
horror
that one might
discover
that perhaps
my body
is what
this person
really wanted.
I, a vessel.
A blood
vessel. I,
a way to
satisfy
and repel. I,
no longer me
but a force.

My only choice
was to stake.
Not intentionally.
But perhaps
Buffy had
prepared me.

Never kill
a human,
of course, Buff.
But how
do I gauge
that state
when I myself
am becoming
meat?

A Paradise of Trombones
For Helen Shivers
I Know What You Did Last Summer (1997)

1.

He must
have swam
back up
to find you.
His whole
death was
spent searching
for you
who accidentally
crowned him
when you
tried to
forget that
your life
was over.

He was
a devoted
fan. He
wanted
to know
just how
long your
blonde hair
fell.

How did you
ever fail?
Carolinaed from
the city
you dreamt
of owning.
The world
was not
ready for
your art.
Your beauty.

You died
at the lip
of your own
salvation.
A paradise
of trombones
waiting
to crest you
into song.

2.

We spend
most of
our time
on land
but water
knew us
first. Water
is the color
of our bodies
when we
move
through it.
Water thieves
the blue
from the sky
in our
absence.
Water is
not itself
and we

are nothing
without it.

Water is
our origin
story. It
swims our
bodies into
flesh. You
are part
water and
light.
Like us
all. You
even in death
were plenished
by water.
Your body
on ice.
Your body
close again
to what
made you.

Haunted House A Go Go
For Daphne Blake
Scooby Doo (2002)

If I could
wear
knee-high
purple boots
today I
would not
be the damsel
in distress
to my own
heartbeat. I'd
be a go go
into the haunted
house where
the armor
would be useless
against my
beauty,

because reflections
can crack
a tooth
but also
stitch
that hole
in our heart
that told us
we would never
be the air
just before
the rainstorm,
that we
would never
be the thick
glut of
desire hanging
like a fruit
on the lip
of our own
quivering
finger confessing

to God that
I am not
Adam or Eve
or Steve,
that I
am a particle
that spins
its own quilt
in the dark
worlds of
this mouth.

With these
boots, I
am the queen
of the
jungleheart,
the go
a go go
into the darkheart
without
any fear

because I've
seen the king
of spades
and he
is weeping
into his own
eyes because he
has found
his own
body guilty
after sliding
his card
under
Alice's skirt
to whisper
"not all men"
to her ankles

and she
swallowed him
like a fruit
and spit

the pit
of him
into the
garden. We

are the hunger
that tides
beneath this
rattlework
and when
these boots
hit the
floor, we
will all be
the most
beautiful
of them all.

THE LANGUAGE OF EYES
FOR JOANNA MILLS
THE RETURN (2006)

Hunted
beneath
the table,
behind
the wood
boards, my
eyes roll
back like
the road
that you
slip
your cowboy
boots on
to escape
from that
little red
memory,

that little
red scar. We
all feel
it, that
heartbeat
under our
skin where
there is
no pulse. We

all try
to sip
the darkness
slowly
enough
so that
it feels
like low
light,
so that
we can
spit out

a sunrise
when people
ask us
how we are,
even though
we know
that sometimes
the only
answers
we have
are the
points
of our pupils
enlarging.

The language
of eyes
is universal.
And I know
that your
green gaze
blues

the sky
the blue
of ghosts
that bring us
to seahorses
painted
on the walls.
To be
haunted

is to be
hunted
by blood
that mimeographs,
and we
are the carbon
copies
of the dawn,
trying
to hide
the fact
that our

parchment
lets in
too much
light.
That we
might fade
if we soak
too much in.

Papercuts blot
our bodies
back into
the red
of mourning.
I sometimes
love
the way
that it feels
to be
in pain.
And I
know you

do too. And
that's when
the ghosts
follow
us

down long
hallways. He
called you
sunshine. My
mother used
to sing
that song
to me—
"you are
my sunshine."
We try
to escape
their violence
through holes
in our flesh.
As if
trying

to purge
ourselves
of their
sunshine,
our soiled
blood.
I know

what it's like
to be
a child
with a bruise.
A child
hiding
beneath
the table.
I know
what it means
to remember
the ghost
inside and I
know
what it means

to heal.

I see you
stare
a million
miles away
and sometimes,
I promise,
I see you.

Lying
in the car
with
or without
breath, we
are the
guardians
of our
bodies. We
just sometimes
forget
how to
love them.

When Your Eyes Close
For Karen Davis
The Grudge (2004)

Your ochre
ghost cracks
an egg
into my
nightmare
and fevers
a demon through
my chest
as the syrup
of time
thwaps
its hair
against my heart
like grenadine
tears in the fabric
of all
the holy

men who
have ever
blessed me.

Why am
I still
this cattle
of glow
sticks weeping
in the dark
while the
children eat
the stars whole
with their eyes
that tumble
death into
galaxies of thick
black rope?

Where do you
go when your
eyes close,

when you
nurse your
body into
trauma and
back again?
When you
succumb to your
haunting of double
hands, a face
pressing through
the flesh
of your dreams?

You are
unaware
of their
eyes watching.
You are
asleep
in the galaxy
of your own
fear. I

slumbered my

whole life

in horror

and now I

speak to you

in tongues

to wake you

to drown out

the tongues

of the children

who slug

the walls

and persuade you

that your

body is

but a memory

of the city you

bury your

fate in.

CRUEL AND DANGEROUS
FOR KATHRYN MURTEUIL
CRUEL INTENTIONS (1999)

1.

It was dangerous
for me
to have a tongue
dangerous
for you
to have a body.
So we became
a rainstorm— me
the puddle, you
the stingray. I
never had
your strength.
Nor your
cruelty. You
could not

separate the two.
Uroburos. You
the sister. You
the smoldering word.

You don't deserve
redemption. But
you do
deserve better
than to
be dragged
down
by the dead
who smilewink
away the crimes
they dump
on you.
I deserve
better too.

I am not
as cruel

as you
but I
easily could
have been.
What
is this world
but bruises,
I think
as you
and I
both weep
into the Hudson
waiting
for the oysters
of our hearts
to shuck
themselves free.

2.

To survive,
you were forced
to be
Marcia Brady.
I am
the broken
nose, and I
have lost
my scent.

So give me
the biggest cross
you have
and I
will snort
it whole. We

are the holy
water. We
are the snuffers
of dreams.

How High
For Cici Cooper
Scream 2 (1997)

1.

Your home
serpentine
a crooked
spine that you
claw into
for safety.
Ghosts flood
our hallways
so that we
mistake the white
light of death
for God. You
clawed deep
into what was
once safety. He

slipped you
deeper into
his mural
of death. Your
body crawling
into fiction. Who

is reading
the novels
our flesh
began? I
have lost my
pen. And you
have lost
your life. I
lost mine long
ago. How
does one
live in a
swallowed
narrative? Someone
chased us both

deep into
the interior
and we
didn't make it
till the end
and we
all know who
did it, saw
them unmasked.
But that will
not resurrect our
old flesh. You
on the pavement. Me
in the theater
watching you
get thrown off
that roof. Having
the dark
desire to
join you.

2.

How high up
would I
need to be
to flood
this novel
and begin
again in a world
where you
and I
could, for once,
be unafraid?

BLOOD OF A CRAB
FOR AMANDA SHELTON
SIMPLY IRRESISTIBLE (1999)

You pour
the flour. Click
the heat. Serve.
And the room
is an hourglass.
And the people
are a flood
of silence. Agape.

Your hair
is red. Mine
is being lost.
I am a hundred
waves burying
my own voice
but the witch
in my bones

elevates me
above this
eternally wet
desert and wipes
my face clean
of its waterfall
as the witch
in your bones
floats
your feet
into the oblivion
of your own
desire.

I am my
own cauldron. I
the bath
of my body.
"Aren't you 29?"
Aww, thanks,
but no
I am

the phoenix
and the phoenix
is dust
years old.

Once someone
told me I
was beautiful
then sprayed
perfume
in my face.
A sample.
On commission.
Paper airplane
in my hair.
Meanwhile, you
wag your finger
in the perfume aisle
and he comes,
beautiful,
his fingers
in his

belt loops.
What is
the recipe
for salvation?
The beak
of me scrawls
its torch
across your menu.
You can use
my dust
in your
next meal. I
can be part
confection. Drop
me into
the cauldron.
Men will
eat me
like air.
But I
will rise
and rise
again.

I am Waiting for You
For Helen Shivers
I Know What You Did Last Summer (1997)

I remember
that dress
but not
the person
in it.
You
are always
swallowed
before I
get the chance
to tell you
about the rain.

Tell me, what
did your
mouth sing
in the only month
of flowers?

I remember
only one
true thing:
the world
is so much
more beautiful
because you
have been
in it.

SHOT OF GELLAR
FOR SARAH MICHELLE GELLAR

I need
a shot
of Gellar
to make it
through
this world
that tells me
stones
are the eyes
of oysters,
tells me
to bite down
and taste
the ocean
in the hard
crust. Everything
tastes better
with a cocktail,

some bourbon,
orange peel.
I'll wash
down a quarry
with a French martini.

A seagull
flew over my
chest while sunning
at Santa Monica.
Its wings beat
my blood
into an egg
and then I
was me
again. Swallow
some sand.
Where's the bartender?

The tides
are a different
color from my

eyes. Shale blue,
ocean view.
That's how
I remember
this world
is actually kind
of beautiful.
Kaleidoscope. Spill
a little bit
of my heart
into a widow's
peaked wave.

So give me
another
and another
but don't
forget me
when the sun
rhinestones.
You see,
my eyes

are Versace.
Please take care
looking
they are a bit
loose. I am
a Gucci robe
without
a body inside
but goddamn
do I sparkle.

What kind
of thread count
are ghosts?
Asking for a friend.

To New Water
For Helen Shivers
I Know What You Did Last Summer (1997)

I caught a galaxy
in my throat
and I'm still
shedding stars.
You, I'm told
were a queen
when we
were still
searching
our nets
for fish. Here,
this constellation
is yours.
Its heat
will body you
out of death.
You can't expire

if you are
part of the
universe. You
are forever
crowned.

He cut
your hair
while you
were sleeping.
I know
what it is like
to be awakened
in the night
with part
of me
missing.
Hair is a metaphor
for the body.
Hair is also
simply beautiful.
And no parts

of our bodies
are anyone's fruit.

I follow
your ambition
to new water.
But I
am always
afraid I
will be found
and outed
for my crimes
only I
have never
committed
a crime.
My only
crime,
like yours,
was to try
to escape
and become

whole. Too
bad you
also pushed
that dead body
into the water.
But perhaps, you
really wished
to be pushing
yours. I
understand that.
But maybe
I'm giving you
too much
credit. Maybe
You really
just drowned
a man.

POSSESSION
FOR JESS
POSSESSION (2009)

1.

A demon
slipped
into my
life
like fish
only
it was never
in me
like I
was told
when I
was shook
free
of Satan
whenever I

disobeyed. I,
legion. I,
pork spilling
from my
wounds.

2.

No, I
am clean.
Here, blow
the wind
through these
holes
from the war
that almost
claimed
my life.

3.

Like yours,
my body
is a hive.
I feel
the sting
sinking into
my skin
as I EMDR
back into
the devil's
backbone.

4.

Sometimes
we want
so badly
to believe
that love
is in
the skin
that hurts us
that we
begin to
crawl
into a
fiction that
blinks
a signal
of safety
to cover
the wreck
that we
are constantly
being pulled
out of.

The Hunt
For Kathryn Murteuil
Cruel Intentions (1999)

1.

Teach me
the hunt.
Teach me not
to burn.
I want
to shed
my vampire.
I want
a body
that hungers
for meat.

Sleep
is a circus
of bones–

my own,
the tooth
of my grandmother.
Are you
more powerful
than my nightmares?
Can you
walk on
their shallows,
raise your cross
and breathe
me in?

2.

I know
you are not
an antidote
but a rabbithole.
If I follow
I might get
swallowed.
But my body
is already missing,
so what is there
to lose
but my fear?

THIS IS NOT A GHOST STORY
FOR JOANNA MILLS
THE RETURN (2006)

My ghost
wolves
the land
looking
for the
lamplight
husking
its glow
about
your face
that slowly
spills
from under
the bed.
So slow
you can
hear

his blood
move
as he
promises
sunshine
if you just
crawl
into sight.

Safety
is a broken
light
we smuggle
our bodies
through,
hoping
traffic
blinks
too fast
to see us.
We are
starfish

in the heat
waiting for
the night
to fling us
toward
the sky
where we
belong.

Whenever
you
remember
your own
ghosts,
you release
your body
to the wind,
let it flow
from you.
But yours
is not
a ghost

story.
It is
evaporation.
How
will I
find you
in this dust
if you
always
planet
your body
toward
God?

A secret
curls in
my hair,
cups
in my
hands.
My ears
rattle

with its
engine.
I am
highwayed
by its heat.
Do you
feel
my heart
beating
where
you are?

I file
a dream
down
with my
nails, insert
it into
my mouth.
Pray
for sweet
dreams.

SO MANY NAMES
FOR BRIDGET KELLY
RINGER (2011)

The one
who shares
your body
tried
to blot
you out
while you
daylighted
as her
to keep
from dying.
But death
clings to you
like your
birthday
necklace,
always
returned.

In the dark
I remember
my
birth
name.
Not I
either,
other I.
I stalks
me. I,
me. Always
an object.

I have
thought
about
changing
my name
because
my body
does not
scrub

clean.
We are
both
stuck
in hallways
of flesh
that remind
us that
we are
not
who we
want
to be.

Your
return
to water
slipped
you
into
an eclipse.
Same

lips, new
secrets.
Even
beautiful
shoes
do not
save you
from
sinking
into
borrowed
skin.

They fell
in love
but not
with you,
only
your
theater.
They never
knew what

they were
missing.

If we
ever meet
I will
hand you
salmon
over
and over
until you
remember
that you
deserve
the ocean.
These
vineyards
are ours.
We will
drink them
in remembrance
of who we
really are.

FOR THOSE WHOSE HORROR WAS LOCKED INSIDE
FOR SARAH MICHELLE GELLAR

"There's no terror in the bang, only
in the anticipation of it"
— Alfred Hitchcock

1.

I often stood
in front
of the mirror
in my mother's
bathroom chanting
Bloody Mary's name.
I longed
for box office
horror. A quick
death. A
wraith sliding
out of the glass

and staining
my body
with my own
blood. Freedom.
Fast. Put me
in the room
with the chainsaws.

When I was
young, my
grandmother often
told me
I was bad.
Locked me
in my room.
"With the devil."
She said
he would heat
it up
so bad
that she
would not

be able
to touch
the door handle
from the other
side. How
to stay safe?
"Pray until
Jesus appears
at the foot
of your bed."

The first few
times she
did this I
prayed so
hard. Then
I stopped.
Let the fire
consume me.
I couldn't
feel it.
But I

wanted to.
Flaming lips.
I did not
want to leave
that room
ever again.
Fire did not
feel
like hell. It
felt like
what would
save me
from it.

2.

My childhood
was a horror
show that all
my friends bought
popcorn for
but they
were there
for a different
type of film.
Family fun.
Endless pizza.
"Your mom
is amazing."
And therein
lies the horror.
To have
my truth
never put
into production.

The film
always burnt
in the room
with me.

3.

Sometimes horror
is quiet.
A hand
where it isn't
supposed to be.
A "don't
tell anyone
or I'll
tell everyone
what a
pervert
you are."
A locked room
where the devil
smokes a pig
roast in my
throat. Sometimes
horror holds
back detail

because it
doesn't give
a shit about
an adrenaline
rush, a jump
scare, but cares
only about
snuffing
a life
and leaving
the body
as bait.

4.

The keyhole
of my life
is taped
over with
whispers. I am
a burnt
offering yet
my skin looks
damn good
with this
Olay cream
and sunscreen.
But crack me
open and my
cooked yolk
is starting
to mold.
Goosebumps
don't always

break
on the flesh
and my heart
is rashed
with all
the ghosts
I have been
and could have been.

This is not
the horror poem
you may be
looking for
because my
blood does not
have a
mouth to
scream with
and my guts
are all
intact. And
nothing howls.

Not anymore.
The world
has quieted.
Yet I have
been the scream
queen,
in the dark,
waiting
for a masked
man to throw
me off
the roof. I,
the scream queen
who never
gets
to die.

The Ending You Deserved
For Helen Shivers
I Know What You Did Last Summer (1997)

In this book
you wear
three crowns,
and you
are finally
the final
girl. You,
the last
lines. You,
bright on
this page,
where you
are as
infinite
as the
night,
and as

beautiful. I
did not
know you
would close
this chapter
for me,
but I
would not
have it
any other
way.

Acknowledgements

I am grateful that poems from this collection have
appeared in the following journals

Drunk Monkeys
Maudlin House
Perhappened
Softblow
Version (9)

Erik Fuhrer is the author of the play *The Ocean and it's Movers* (Free Lines Press) and six previous collections of poetry: *Eye, Apocalypse, in which I take myself hostage* (Spuyten Duyvil), *At Root, every time I die* (Alien Buddha), *VOS* (Yavanika), and *not human enough for the census* (Vegetarian Alcoholic). Their memoir, *My Buffed Up Life*, which engages with *Buffy the Vampire Slayer* to unfold an otherwise unspeakable tale of personal trauma, is forthcoming from Spuyten Duyvil Press in 2024. They hold a PhD from The University of Glasgow and currently live and teach in Los Angeles.